ETHIOPIA

By Jagger Youssef and
Nancy DiStasio

EXPLORING WORLD CULTURES

Cavendish Square

Published in 2027 by Cavendish Square Publishing, LLC
2544 Clinton Street, Buffalo, NY 14224

Second Edition

Website: cavendishsq.com

Library of Congress Cataloging-in-Publication Data

Names: Youssef, Jagger author | DiStasio, Nancy author
Title: Ethiopia / Jagger Youssef and Nancy DiStasio.
Other titles: Exploring world cultures
Description: New York : Cavendish Square Publishing, 2026. | Series: Exploring world cultures | Includes index. | Audience: Grades 2-3
Identifiers: LCCN 2026004488 (print) | LCCN 2026004489 (ebook) | ISBN 9781502677143 library binding | ISBN 9781502677136 paperback | ISBN 9781502677150 ebook
Subjects: LCSH: Ethiopia | Africa | LCGFT: Literature
Classification: LCC DT373 .Y68 2026 (print) | LCC DT373 (ebook) | DDC 963--dc23/eng/20260223
LC record available at https://lccn.loc.gov/2026004488
LC ebook record available at https://lccn.loc.gov/2026004489

Writers: Jagger Youssef, Nancy DiStasio (second edition)
Editor: Therese Shea
Designer: Deanna Lepovich

The photographs in this book are used by permission and through the courtesy of: Cover Riccardo Mayer/Shutterstock.com; p. 4 GRANT ROONEY PREMIUM/Alamy Photos; p. 5 Rainer Lesniewski/Shutterstock.com; p. 7 (top) Matyas Rehak/Shutterstock.com; p. 7 (bottom) Mikhail Cheremkin/Shutterstock.com; p. 8 Chronicle/Alamy Photos; p. 9 Neil McAllister/Alamy Photos; p. 10 zmotions/Shutterstock.com; p. 11 PorcupenWorks/Shutterstock.com; p. 12 Hybrid_Production Ethiopia/Shutterstock.com; p. 13 Eric Isselee/Shutterstock.com; p. 14 Vlad Karavaev/Shutterstock.com; p. 15 Artush/Shutterstock.com; p. 16 Roberto Fumagalli/Alamy Photos; p. 17 enisey/Shutterstock.com; p. 18 Artush/Shutterstock.com; p. 19 AleCasa77/Shutterstock.com; p. 20 ERIC LAFFORGUE/Alamy Photos; p. 21 Mile 91/Ben Langdon/Alamy Photos; p. 22 History and Art Collection/Alamy Photos; p. 23 rvdw images/Shutterstock.com; p. 24 fekadu/Shutterstock.com; p. 25 Framalicious/Shutterstock.com; p. 27 (top) Maxisport/Shutterstock.com; p. 27 (bottom) dpa picture alliance/Alamy Photos; p. 28 Alvi Prasetya/Shutterstock.com; p. 29 MagicBones/Shutterstock.com.

CPSIA compliance information: Batch #CS27CSQ: For further information contact Cavendish Square Publishing LLC at 1-877-980-4450.

Printed in United States of America

CONTENTS

INTRODUCTION

Ethiopia is the oldest independent, or free, African nation. It's also one of the largest African countries. In addition, Ethiopia is the second most **populated** country with more than 118 million people. Ethiopians aren't a single people, however, but are many **ethnicities**, with different beliefs and ways of life.

Ethiopia has many kinds of land features, including mountains, plains, forests, grasslands, and deserts. Some parts of the nation are hot, while others are cooler.

Many peoples in Ethiopia have long histories and long-practiced customs, or ways of life.

Most Ethiopians live in rural, or country, areas, where they try to grow their own food and raise animals. Some live in cities, including the nation's capital city of Addis Ababa. Other cities include Dire Dawa and Bahir Dar.

Though the people work hard, Ethiopia is one of the poorest countries in the world. Many people have a hard time getting enough food and clean water to live. This is a problem the country's government continues to try to fix.

In this photo, you can see that Ethiopia is a landlocked country. This is a word that means it doesn't touch an ocean.

GEOGRAPHY

Ethiopia is surrounded by many nations. These include Eritrea, Djibouti, Somalia, Kenya, South Sudan, and Sudan. Ethiopia is located in a part of eastern Africa known as the Horn of Africa.

Ethiopia's landscape has mountains and a plateau, which is an area of high, flat land. It also has lowlands that sit below sea level. The East African Rift System, which includes the Great Rift Valley, cuts through Ethiopia. It's made up of many trenches, or deep and narrow cuts in Earth's surface.

Ethiopia has rivers and lakes, as well as dry deserts. Most parts of Ethiopia have a wet and dry season each year. Some areas, however, are more likely to have **drought**.

FACT!

Ethiopia's highest mountain is Ras Dashen, which is 14,930 feet (4,550 meters).

Rainfall is important to all Ethiopians, not just farmers.

*The East African Rift System is still active today. The moving plates cause **earthquakes** and **volcanic eruptions**.*

A BIG SPLIT

The East African Rift System is where a tectonic plate called the African plate is splitting apart. Tectonic plates are large pieces of rock that make up Earth's outer layer.

HISTORY

Scientists have long been interested in Ethiopia. They have found remains there of human **ancestors** and early modern humans. Over time, people began to settle in Ethiopia. Around 100 CE, the powerful kingdom of Aksum began there.

Throughout history, outsiders wanted to own Ethiopia, but they were unsuccessful. From 1936 to 1941, Italy tried to control Ethiopia, but failed.

Ethiopia was once ruled by emperors who had total power over the people. In 1995, a new constitution, or set of laws, went into effect. Ethiopians had a bigger say and voted in elections.

Haile Selassie was the emperor of Ethiopia from 1930 until 1974.

Some parts of Ethiopia have monuments from the past, such as this stela, or column, in Aksum (or Axum). It dates from the 300s CE.

The border between Ethiopia and Eritrea was fought over for many years, until 2018. Conflicts, or fights, between the Ethiopian government and people in the northern Tigray area of the country continue.

FACT!

Ethiopia is the only African country that has never been a colony. A colony is land under the control of another country.

FINDING LUCY

One of the most famous human ancestors found in Ethiopia was a female who lived more than 3 million years ago. Scientists nicknamed her Lucy.

GOVERNMENT

Ethiopia's government has changed over time. Today, it has a national government with three branches—much like the U.S. government has. The Ethiopian government is centered in the capital, Addis Ababa.

The legislative branch, or parliament, makes the laws. The executive branch includes a president, who serves as the head of state. This means they represent, or stand for, Ethiopia on the world stage. The president has little power, however. The prime minister is the main leader of the government. Abiy Ahmed Ali has served as prime minister of Ethiopia since 2018.

*On the flag of Ethiopia, the star represents, or stands for, the Ethiopian peoples. Yellow represents hope, red represents **sacrifice**, and green represents the land.*

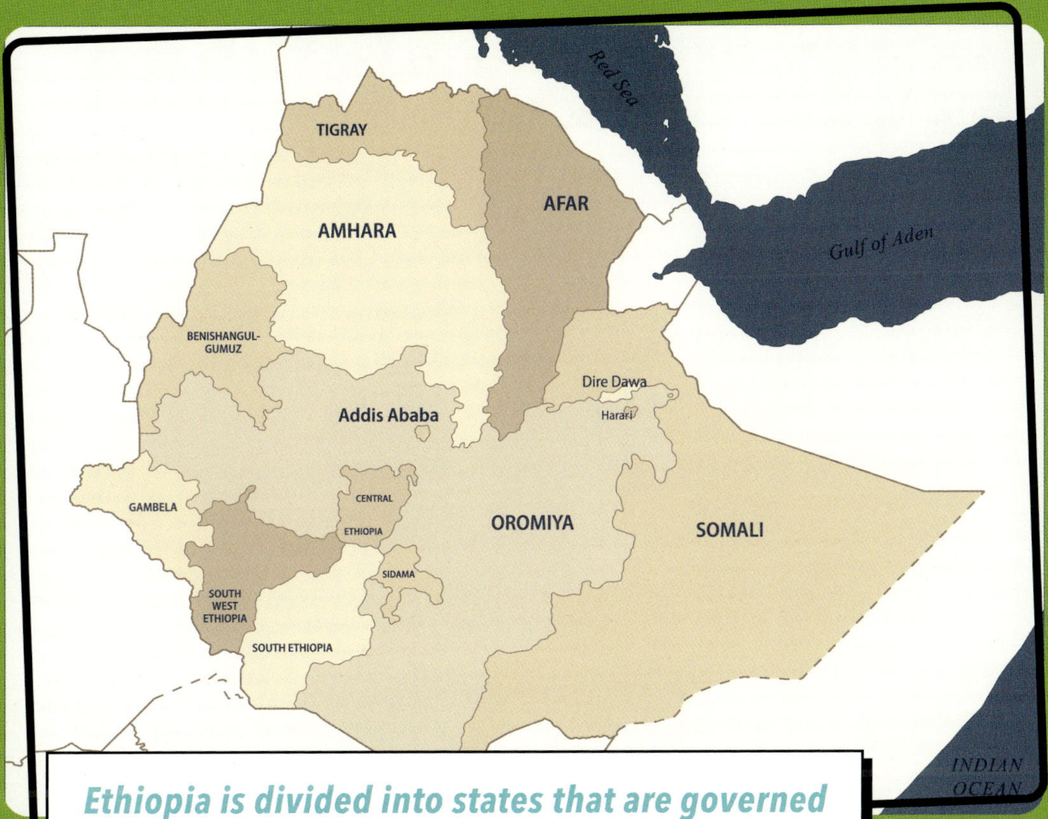

Ethiopia is divided into states that are governed by groups of leaders called councils.

The courts make up the judicial branch of the Ethiopian government. Judges can serve until they are 65 years old. The highest court is the Federal Supreme Court.

A FIRST

In 2018, Sahle-Work Zewde became Ethiopia's first female president. She served until 2024.

THE ECONOMY

The Ethiopian **economy** depends mainly on agriculture, or raising crops and animals. Most people who live in the country are farmers. However, it's sometimes hard to grow crops. The soil can be poor. Droughts slow or stop plant growth. But some areas of the country often have good crops, including grains, coffee, and vegetables. Ethiopians also raise livestock such as cattle, sheep, goats, camels, and chickens.

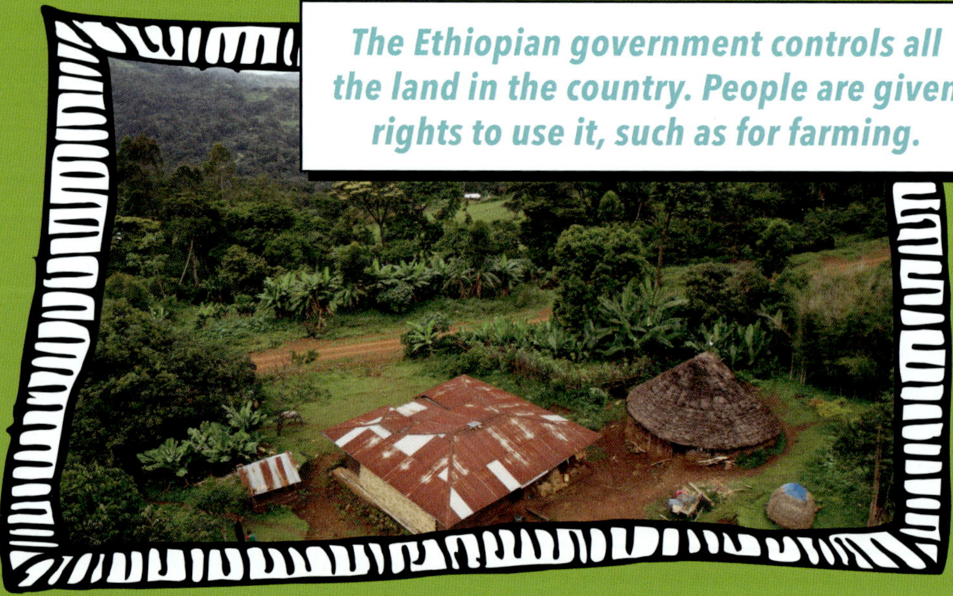

The Ethiopian government controls all the land in the country. People are given rights to use it, such as for farming.

People who live in Ethiopia's cities do different kinds of jobs. Some have service jobs, such as working in hospitals or hotels. Factory workers make clothing and other goods.

Many Ethiopians are very poor. Other countries and groups sometimes aid the poorest people, but Ethiopia remains one of the poorest countries in the world.

FACT!

Ethiopia has mines, including for salt, gold, and other ***minerals****.*

Ethiopia's most important export is coffee. An export is something sold to another country.

THE BIRR

The birr is the basic unit of Ethiopian money. It's divided into 100 santims.

THE ENVIRONMENT

Ethiopia has beautiful areas of nature. It's home to many animals too, such as lions, elephants, and giraffes. However, Ethiopia also has environmental problems, or problems dealing with nature.

Many Ethiopians are living without **access** to clean, safe drinking water. Water from rivers can be dirty and make people sick. In some places, people have to walk a long way to get fresh, clean water to drink.

Desertification is the turning of good soil into dry, poor soil. This can happen because of overfarming and the cutting down of trees. It's a big problem in Ethiopia.

In 2015, Ethiopia began a terrible drought. The lack of rain led to poor crops and less drinking water. In 2020, locusts attacked parts of the country. This kind of grasshopper destroyed crops. Some people had to leave their homes.

In recent years, the government has tried to act for a better future. For example, the government plans to plant billions of trees to replace cut-down forests.

FACT!

Simien National Park is one of Ethiopia's many national parks.

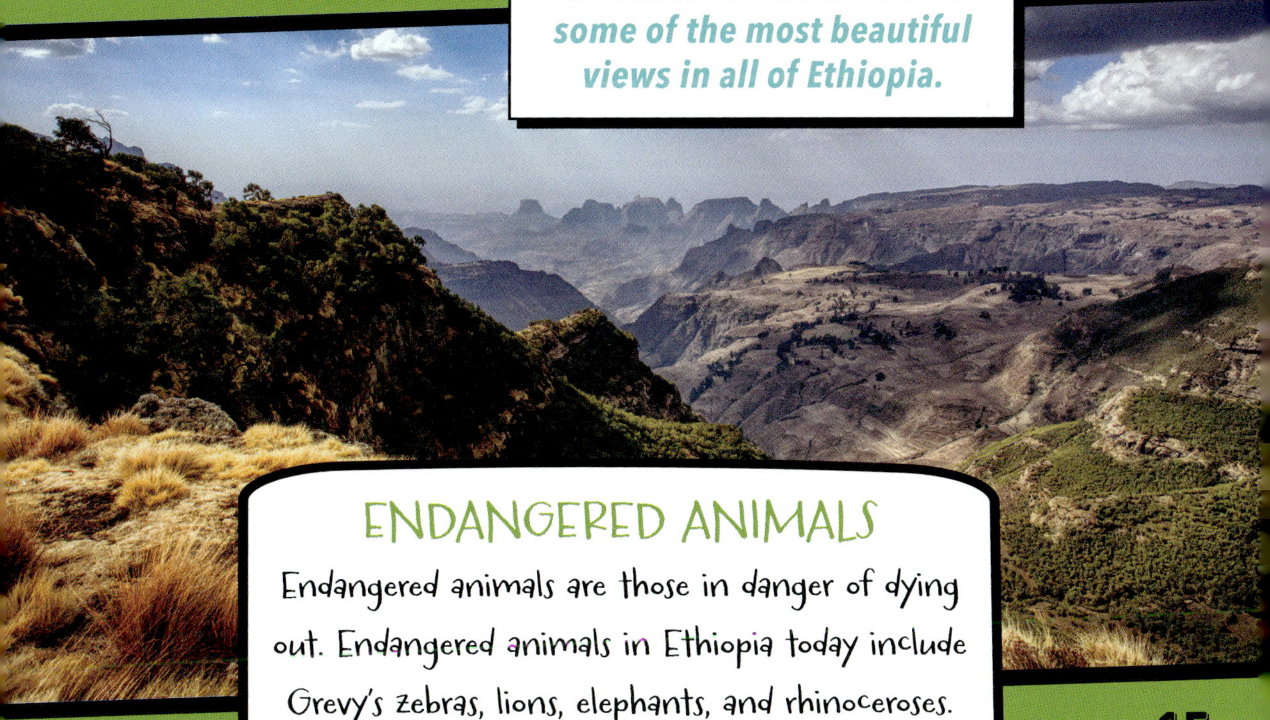

The Simien Mountains offer some of the most beautiful views in all of Ethiopia.

ENDANGERED ANIMALS

Endangered animals are those in danger of dying out. Endangered animals in Ethiopia today include Grevy's zebras, lions, elephants, and rhinoceroses.

THE PEOPLE TODAY

As of 2024, about 118 million people lived in Ethiopia. Only one other country in Africa has more people living in it—Nigeria. Most of Ethiopia's people are young. About half of all Ethiopians are children or teenagers. Ethiopia's population is also growing quickly. Women in this country often have many children. Large families sometimes cannot get the food and water they need.

FACT!

Most Ethiopians live in the north and central areas of the country. Fewer live in the east and south.

These girls are wearing Oromo kinds of dress.

Ethiopia is made up of around 80 different ethnicities. Many belong to the Oromo, Amhara, Somali, and Tigray ethnic groups. People in an ethnic group often have common languages and customs.

Most Ethiopians live in rural areas, but nearly one-fourth live in cities. The city of Addis Ababa is the largest, with more than 5 million people.

Almost 40 percent of Ethiopia's people are 14 years old or younger.

FATHER'S NAME

Ethiopian children are given a first name when they're born. Their father's first name becomes their last name.

LIFESTYLE

About 80 percent of all Ethiopians live in rural areas of the nation. Rural people get around by mostly walking or riding animals, not by car. Homes in rural Ethiopia are simple. Some are built from wood and mud. Others are made from stone.

Some Ethiopians leave the countryside to try to build a better life in a city. They hope to make more money and go to better schools. Many cities in Ethiopia offer higher paying jobs, cleaner water, and electricity, which rural areas often don't have.

People walk into the town of Demebecha in northern Ethiopia.

In Ethiopia, rural women and children often have the job of carrying water or wood to their homes. Sometimes this takes hours.

Many Ethiopian children are busy helping on farms or taking care of younger brothers or sisters. This makes it hard for them to attend school. They often miss school and don't go on to higher grades.

FACT!
In rural areas, Ethiopians may not get health care they need.

SCHOOL PROBLEMS

A bit more than half of adult Ethiopians can read and write. Others cannot because they had to take care of families or farms rather than go to school. Still others lived too far from schools.

RELIGION

More than half of Ethiopians are Christians. Christians are people who follow the teachings of Jesus Christ. The Ethiopian Orthodox Tewahedo Church is the kind of Christianity there with the most followers. Other Ethiopian Christians are Protestants or Roman Catholics. Important holidays they all celebrate include Christmas and Easter.

About one-third of the Ethiopian population is Muslim. They follow the teachings of Muhammad. There are smaller groups of people who practice other religions.

These Ethiopian Orthodox priests are holding a special celebration.

Some Ethiopians practice traditional African religions—ones that have been passed down over centuries. These religions existed long before Christianity came to Ethiopia. A small number of Ethiopians follow a belief system called animism. Animists believe all things, including parts of the natural world and human-made objects, have a spirit. Some people blend beliefs in different faiths.

EARLY AFRICAN CHURCH

The Ethiopian Orthodox Tewahedo Church dates back to the Kingdom of Aksum in Ethiopia and Eritrea. Christianity took root there in 330 CE.

FACT!

Many Ethiopian Jews left the nation and moved to Israel.

Ethiopia has many beautiful mosques, which are buildings where Muslims worship.

LANGUAGE

Close to 100 languages are spoken in Ethiopia. An Ethiopian's ethnic background and location plays a part in the language they speak. The government recognizes all Ethiopian languages. Oromo is the most common language spoken, but Amharic is often called the country's official national language and is the "working language" of the government.

The Ethiopian Orthodox Tewahedo Church still uses the Ge'ez language in its rituals, or religious events, and in its writings.

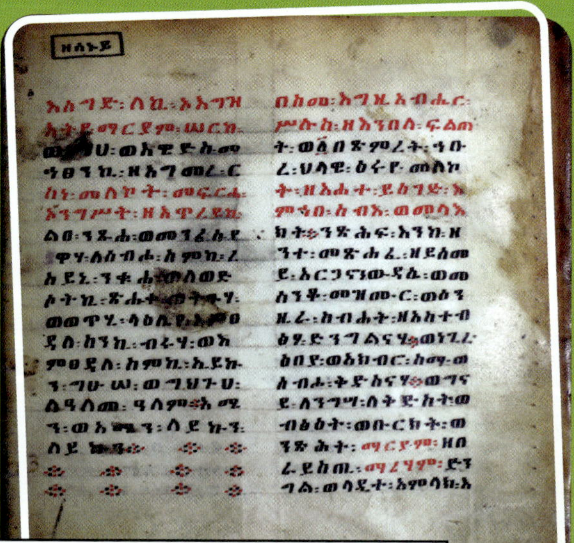

Ge'ez is a very old language from the past that's still part of life for some Ethiopian Christians.

Many Ethiopians speak more than one language. Children who attend school learn English. This makes it one of the most spoken foreign, or outside, languages. Many Muslim Ethiopians are able to speak Arabic because of their religion as well.

FACT!

A few languages in Ethiopia are close to becoming extinct, or going out of use.

The Amharic language uses a writing system in which a character, or symbol, represents a consonant and a vowel syllable.

GE'EZ

Ge'ez isn't spoken outside of religious use. It's sometimes called a "dead language" because it's not used in daily life anymore.

ARTS AND FESTIVALS

Music and other arts have long been a key part of Ethiopian **cultures**. Many Ethiopian musicians use traditional instruments to play traditional songs. Brass bands have also become popular in this country.

Ethiopians perform, or take part in, plays. Theater festivals take place where plays are performed for the public.

FACT!
Adwa Victory Day is celebrated on March 2 in Ethiopia. It marks the 1896 Ethiopian victory over Italian forces at the Battle of Adwa.

Ethiopians march in a parade to celebrate Adwa Victory Day.

Timket (or Timkat) is celebrated around January 19. In some places, such as Gonder, people gather near water to celebrate the baptism of Jesus.

Many kinds of Ethiopian celebrations are based on religion. Timket, or the Feast of the Epiphany, is celebrated in January by the Ethiopian Orthodox Tewahedo Church. It honors the baptism of Jesus, which is when he washed in the Jordan River before he started preaching. Meskel takes place at the end of September. It celebrates the finding of the cross that Jesus died on. Ethiopian Orthodox Christians celebrate Christmas on January 7 rather than December 25.

NEW YEAR CELEBRATION

The Ethiopian New Year is called Enkutatash. It often falls on September 11.

FUN AND PLAY

Life in Ethiopia includes games and sports, especially for children. Some popular ones include *gebeta*, a board game, and *segno maksegno*, which is a form of hopscotch. *Yegena chewata* is like field hockey and is commonly played around Christmas. Ethiopians often play this game with homemade sticks and balls. Games and sports often use things that children make or find rather than buy.

Running is a part of the Ethiopian way of life. The country produces some of the fastest long-distance runners in the world. About 40,000 people take part in the Great Ethiopian Run every year. It takes place in Addis Ababa. Runners in this 10-kilometer (about 6 miles) race include famous Ethiopians and visitors from all over the world.

OLYMPIC SUCCESS

As of 2026, Ethiopia has won 58 Olympic medals, all in track and field events. Twenty-three of these were gold medals.

Ethiopians have long been successful at the Olympic Games in running sports.

FACT!

The Ethiopian town of Bekoji has produced so many successful runners that it has been called "the fastest place on Earth."

The most popular sport in Ethiopia is soccer, which is called football in many parts of the world.

FOOD

Ethiopian food is known for its interesting seasonings. One dish is a kind of stew called wat, or wot. It may contain meat, **lentils**, or chickpeas as well as vegetables. A mix of spices called berbere may flavor it.

The Ethiopian coffee ritual is called the Habesha coffee ceremony.

COFFEE CEREMONY

Coffee is served in a special way each day. The coffee beans are roasted over a fire. Then, they are ground and added to hot water. People chat about their day while the coffee is prepared.

Coffee and tea are both important drinks in Ethiopia. Meals often don't need forks and spoons. Instead, people rip pieces of a flat thin bread called injera and use these to scoop up what they eat. People may feed each other bites of food out of respect, love, or friendship.

Many cities around the world have Ethiopian restaurants. Going to one is a great way to connect with an important part of Ethiopian culture.

FACT!

Ethiopians only use their right hand to pick up food and eat.

In this photo, you can see several vegetarian dishes as well as the injera bread they will be eaten with.

GLOSSARY

access: The ability to use or have something.

ancestor: An animal that lived before others in its family tree.

culture: The beliefs and ways of life of a group of people.

drought: A long period of very dry weather.

earthquake: A shaking of the ground caused by the movement of Earth's crust.

economy: The money made in an area and how it is made.

ethnicity: A part of a person's identity based on where they or their family come from.

lentil: A seed from a plant in the pea family that can be eaten.

mineral: Matter in the ground that forms rocks.

populated: Having people.

sacrifice: A giving up of something, which allows someone else to receive something.

syllable: The individual sounds that make up a word in spoken language.

volcanic eruption: The bursting forth of hot, liquid rock from within Earth.

FIND OUT MORE

Books

Bell, Samantha. *Ethiopia*. Mendota Heights, MN: Focus Readers, 2025.

Klepeis, Alicia. *Ethiopia*. Minneapolis, MN: Bellwether Media, 2023.

Websites

Ethiopia
kids.britannica.com/kids/article/Ethiopia/345687
Britannica Kids provides a review of facts about this country.

Facts About Ethiopia
kids-world-travel-guide.com/facts-about-ethiopia.html
This site has more photos and information about Ethiopia.

Video

Ethiopia
www.globetrottinkids.com/countries/ethiopia/
This website has a video about Ethiopia made just for kids.

INDEX